Advices
Queries &

A compilation of
Australian and British
Advices and Queries

Australia Yearly Meeting
Religious Society of Friends in Australia

© Australia Yearly Meeting of the
Religious Society of Friends in Australia
PO Box 556, Kenmore, Queensland 4069

First published 2008
Reprinted 2009, 2015

National Library of Australia
Cataloguing-in-Publication data:

Advices and queries: a compilation of
Australian and British advices and queries
/ Religious Society of Friends in Australia.

ISBN 9780975157954 (pbk.)

Subjects:
Religious thought.
Christian life--Biblical teaching.
Society of Friends.
Religious Society of Friends (Quakers) in Australia.

Dewey: 230.01

Distributed in physical and eBook versions by:

IP (Interactive Publications Pty Ltd)
Treetop Studio, 9 Kuhler Ct.
Carindale, Queensland
Australia 4152
http://ipoz.biz/ipstore
sales@ipoz.biz

Introduction

As Friends we commit ourselves to a way of worship which allows God to teach and transform us. We have found corporately that the Spirit, if rightly followed, will lead us into truth, unity and love: all our testimonies grow from this leading.

Although the corporate use of advices and queries is governed by more flexible regulations than in the past, they should continue to be a challenge and inspiration to Friends in their personal lives and in their life as a religious community which knows the guidance of the universal spirit of Christ, witnessed to in the life and teachings of Jesus of Nazareth.

Advices and queries are not a call to increased activity by each individual Friend but a reminder of the insights of the Society. Within the community there is a diversity of gifts. We are all therefore asked to consider how far the advices and queries affect us personally and where our own service lies. There will also be diversity of experience, of belief and of language. Friends maintain that expressions of faith must be related to personal experience. Some find traditional Christian language full of meaning; some do not. Our understanding of our own religious tradition may sometimes be enhanced by insights of other faiths. The deeper realities of our faith are beyond precise verbal formulation and our way of worship based on silent waiting testifies to this.

Our diversity invites us both to speak what we know to be true in our lives and to learn from others. Friends are encouraged to listen to each other in humility and understanding, trusting in the Spirit that goes beyond our human effort and comprehension. So it is for the comfort and discomfort of Friends that these advices and queries are offered, with the hope that we may all be more faithful and find deeper joy in God's service.

Dearly beloved Friends, these things we do not lay upon you as a rule or form to walk by, but that all, with the measure of light which is pure and holy, may be guided; and so in the light walking and abiding, these may be fulfilled in the Spirit, not from the letter, for the letter killeth, but the Spirit giveth life.

Postscript to an epistle to 'the brethren in the north' issued by a meeting of elders at Balby, 1656

1 Take heed, dear Friends, to the promptings of love and truth in your hearts. Trust them as the leadings of God whose Light shows us our darkness and brings us to new life.

2 Bring the whole of your life under the ordering of the spirit of Christ. Are you open to the healing power of God's love? Cherish that of God within you, so that this love may grow in you and guide you. Let your worship and your daily life enrich each other. Treasure your experience of God, however it comes to you. Remember that Christianity is not a notion but a way.

3 Do you try to set aside times of quiet for openness to the Holy Spirit? All of us need to find a way into silence which allows us to deepen our awareness of the divine and to find the inward source of our strength. Seek to know an inward stillness, even amid the activities of daily life. Do you encourage in yourself and in others a habit of dependence on God's guidance for each day? Hold yourself and others in the Light, knowing that all are cherished by God.

4 The Religious Society of Friends is rooted in Christianity and has always found inspiration in the life and teachings of Jesus. How do

3

you interpret your faith in the light of this heritage? How does Jesus speak to you today? Are you following Jesus' example of love in action? Are you learning from his life the reality and cost of obedience to God? How does his relationship with God challenge and inspire you?

5 Take time to learn about other people's experiences of the Light. Remember the importance of the Bible, the writings of Friends and all writings which reveal the ways of God. As you learn from others, can you in turn give freely from what you have gained? While respecting the experiences and opinions of others, do

not be afraid to say what you have found and what you value. Appreciate that doubt and questioning can also lead to spiritual growth and to a greater awareness of the Light that is in us all.

6 Do you work gladly with other religious groups in the pursuit of common goals? While remaining faithful to Quaker insights, try to enter imaginatively into the life and witness of other communities of faith, creating together the bonds of friendship.

7 Be aware of the spirit of God at work in the ordinary activities and experience of your daily life.

Spiritual learning continues throughout life, and often in unexpected ways. There is inspiration to be found all around us, in the natural world, in the sciences and arts, in our work and friendships, in our sorrows as well as in our joys. Are you open to new light, from whatever source it may come? Do you approach new ideas with discernment?

8 We are excited by the accelerating development of scientific knowledge, and mindful of both the benefits and the horrors this may bring. Let us remember that the universe shown to us by the sciences is a divine gift, and not turn away from our responsibility to consider the implications of scientific and technical discoveries.

9 Worship is our response to an awareness of God. We can worship alone, but when we join with others in expectant waiting we may discover a deeper sense of God's presence. We seek a gathered stillness in our meetings for worship so that all may feel the power of God's love drawing us together and leading us.

10 In worship we enter with reverence into communion with God and respond to the promptings of the Holy Spirit. Come to meeting for worship with heart and mind prepared.

Yield yourself and all your outward concerns to God's guidance so that you may find "the evil weakening in you and the good raised up".

11 Come regularly to meeting for worship even when you are angry, depressed, tired or spiritually cold. In the silence ask for and accept the prayerful support of others joined with you in worship. Try to find a spiritual wholeness which encompasses suffering as well as thankfulness and joy. Prayer, springing from a deep place in the heart, may bring healing and unity as nothing else can. Let meeting for worship nourish your whole life.

12 Be honest with yourself. What unpalatable truths might you be evading? When you recognise your shortcomings, do not let that discourage you. In worship together we can find the assurance of God's love and the strength to go on with renewed courage.

13 When you are preoccupied and distracted in meeting let wayward and disturbing thoughts give way quietly to your awareness of God's presence among us and in the world. Receive the vocal ministry of others in a tender and creative spirit. Reach for the meaning deep within it, recognising that even if it is not God's

word for you, it may be so for others. Remember that we all share responsibility for the meeting for worship whether our ministry is in silence or through the spoken word.

14 Do not assume that vocal ministry is never to be your part. Faithfulness and sincerity in speaking, even very briefly, may open the way to fuller ministry from others. When prompted to speak, wait patiently to know that the leading and the time are right, but do not let a sense of your own unworthiness hold you back. Pray that your ministry may arise from deep experience, and trust that words will be given to you. Try to speak audibly and distinctly, and with sensitivity to the needs of others. Beware of speaking predictably or too often, and of making additions towards the end of a meeting when it was well left before.

15 Are your meetings for church affairs held in a spirit of worship and in dependence on the guidance of God? Remember that we do not seek a majority decision nor even consensus. As we wait patiently for divine guidance our experience is that the right way will open and we shall be led into unity.

16 Do you take part as often as you can in meetings for church affairs? Are you familiar enough with our church government to contribute to its disciplined processes? Do you consider difficult questions with an informed mind as well as a generous and loving spirit? Are you prepared to let your insights and personal wishes take their place alongside those of others or be set aside as the meeting seeks the right way forward? If you cannot attend, uphold the meeting prayerfully.

17 Do you welcome the diversity of culture, language and expressions of faith in our yearly meeting and in the world community of Friends? Seek to increase your understanding and to gain from this rich heritage and wide range of spiritual insights. Uphold your own and other yearly meetings in your prayers.

18 For thousands of years before 1788, this country was lived in by various Aboriginal peoples, at one with the land. Through colonisation, much of their land and culture has been lost to them, and their children have been taken from them; they have suffered the injustice of racism, and material, psychological and spiritual deprivation. Can we acknowledge with sorrow the loss of life and the on-going destruction of their languages, families and communities, appreciate the depth and strength of Aboriginal beliefs and values and learn from Aboriginal people and accept the gifts they have for all of us? Can we all, as Australians, work towards living together as equals, with mutual understanding and respect?

19 Do you respect that of God in everyone though it may be expressed in unfamiliar ways or be difficult to discern? Each of us has a particular experience of God and each must find the way to be true to it. When words are strange or disturbing to you, try to sense where they

come from and what has nourished the lives of others. Listen patiently and seek the truth which other people's opinions may contain for you. Avoid hurtful criticism and provocative language. Do not allow the strength of your convictions to betray you into making statements or allegations that are unfair or untrue. Think it possible that you may be mistaken.

20 How can we make the meeting a community in which each person is accepted and nurtured, and strangers are welcome? Seek to know one another in the things which are eternal, bear the burden of each other's failings and pray for one another. As we enter with tender sympathy into the joys and sorrows of each other's lives, ready to give help and to receive it, our meeting can be a channel for God's love and forgiveness.

21 Rejoice in the presence of children and young people in your meeting and recognise the gifts they bring. Remember that the meeting as a whole shares a responsibility for every child in its care. Seek for them as for yourself a full development of God's gifts and the abundant life Jesus tells us can be ours. How do you share your deepest beliefs with them, while leaving them free to develop as the spirit of God may lead

them? Do you invite them to share their insights with you? Are you ready both to learn from them and to accept your responsibilities towards them?

22 Do you give sufficient time to sharing with others in the meeting, both newcomers and long-time members, your understanding of worship, of service, and of commitment to the Society's witness? Do you give a right proportion of your money to support Quaker work?

23 Do you cherish your friendships, so that they grow in depth and understanding and mutual respect? In close relationships we may risk pain as well as finding joy. When experiencing great happiness or great hurt we may be more open to the working of the Spirit.

24 Respect the wide diversity among us in our lives and relationships. Refrain from making prejudiced judgments about the life journeys of others. Do you foster the spirit of mutual understanding and forgiveness which our discipleship asks of us? Remember that each one of us is unique, precious, a child of God.

25 Marriage has always been regarded by Friends as a religious commitment rather than a merely civil contract. Both partners should offer with God's help an intention to cherish one another for life. Remember that happiness depends on an understanding and steadfast love on both sides. In times of difficulty remind yourself of the value of prayer, of perseverance and of a sense of humour.

26 Children and young people need love and stability. Are we doing all we can to uphold and sustain parents and others who carry the responsibility for providing this care?

27 A long-term relationship brings tensions as well as fulfilment. If your relationship with your partner is under strain, seek help in understanding the other's point of view and in exploring your own feelings, which may be powerful and destructive. Consider the wishes and feelings of any children involved, and remember their enduring need for love and security. Seek God's guidance. If you undergo the distress of separation or divorce, try to maintain some compassionate communication so that arrangements can be made with the minimum of bitterness.

28 Do you recognise the needs and gifts of each member of your family and household, not forgetting your own? Try to make your home a place of loving friendship and enjoyment, where all who live or visit may find the peace and refreshment of God's presence.

29 Live adventurously. When choices arise, do you take the way that offers the fullest opportunity for the use of your gifts in the service of God and the community? Let your life speak. When decisions have to be made, are you ready to join with others in seeking clearness, asking for God's guidance and offering counsel to one another?

30 Every stage of our lives offers fresh opportunities. Responding to divine guidance, try to discern the right time to undertake or relinquish responsibilities without undue pride or guilt. Attend to what love requires of you, which may not be great busyness.

31 Approach old age with courage and hope. As far as possible, make arrangements for your care in good time, so that an undue burden does not fall on others. Although old age may bring increasing disability and loneliness, it can also bring serenity, detachment and wisdom. Pray that in your final years you may be enabled to find new ways of receiving and reflecting God's love.

32 Are you able to contemplate your death and the death of those closest to you? Accepting the fact of death, we are freed to live more fully. In bereavement, give yourself time to grieve. When others mourn, let your love embrace them.

33 We are called to live "in the virtue of that life and power that takes away the occasion of all wars". Do you faithfully maintain our testimony that war and the preparation for war are inconsistent with the spirit of Christ? Search out whatever in your own way of life may contain the seeds of war. Stand firm in our testimony, even when others commit or prepare to commit acts of violence, yet always remember that they too are children of God.

34 Bring into God's light those emotions, attitudes and prejudices in yourself which lie at the root of destructive conflict, acknowledging your need for forgiveness and grace. In what ways are you involved in the work of reconciliation between individuals, groups and nations?

35 Within Australia and in neighbouring countries, people of goodwill seek to know and to worship God in ways other than those of Christianity. Do we listen to their insights with open hearts and minds, recognising that we do not possess all the Truth, but only a part of it? Do we think of these neighbours with acceptance? Do we seek knowledge and understanding of their beliefs and the Light which is theirs?

36 Are you alert to practices here and throughout the world which discriminate against people on the basis of who or what they are or because of their

beliefs? Bear witness to the humanity of all people, including those who break society's conventions or its laws. Try to discern new growing points in social and economic life. Seek to understand the causes of injustice, social unrest and fear. Are you working to bring about a just and compassionate society which allows everyone to develop their capacities and fosters the desire to serve?

37 Remember your responsibilities as a citizen for the conduct of local, national, and international affairs. Do not shrink from the time and effort your involvement may demand.

38 Respect the laws of the state but let your first loyalty be to God's purposes. If you feel impelled by strong conviction to break the law, search your conscience deeply. Ask your meeting for the prayerful support which will give you strength as a right way becomes clear.

39 Do you uphold those who are acting under concern, even if their way is not yours? Can you lay aside your own wishes and prejudices while seeking with others to find God's will for them?

40 Are you honest and truthful in all you say and

do? Do you maintain strict integrity in business transactions and in your dealings with individuals and organisations? Do you use money and information entrusted to you with discretion and responsibility? Taking oaths implies a double standard of truth; in choosing to affirm instead, be aware of the claim to integrity that you are making.

41 If pressure is brought upon you to lower your standard of integrity, are you prepared to resist it? Our responsibilities to God and our neighbour may involve us in taking unpopular stands. Do not let the desire to be sociable, or the fear of seeming peculiar,

determine your decisions.

42 Consider which of the ways to happiness offered by society are truly fulfilling and which are potentially corrupting and destructive. Be discriminating when choosing means of entertainment and information. Resist the desire to acquire possessions or income through unethical investment, speculation or games of chance.

43 In view of the harm done by the use of alcohol, tobacco and other habit-forming drugs, consider whether you should limit your use of them or refrain from using them altogether. Remember that any use of alcohol or drugs may impair judgment and put both the user and others in danger.

44 All life is inter-related. Each individual plant and animal has its own needs, and is important to others. Many Australian species, and other species worldwide, are now extinct, and countless more are endangered. Do you treat all life with respect, recognising a particular obligation to those animals we breed and maintain for our own use and enjoyment? In order to secure the survival of all, including ourselves, are you prepared to change your ideas about your relationship to your environment and every living thing in it?

45 Try to live simply. A simple lifestyle freely chosen is a source of strength. Do not be persuaded into buying what you do not need or cannot afford. Do you keep yourself informed about the effects your style of living is having on the global economy and environment?

46 The land of Australia is not our possession. We are no more than temporary guardians of it; neither the first nor, probably, the last. In the brief time of European settlement, vast areas of this country have

been damaged. Do you try to live in harmony with the land, knowing that you are part of it? Do you protect and husband its water and other resources? Do you look with respect on the claims and rights of others to share in the wealth and freedoms of Australians?

47 We live in a land of unique grandeur and beauty, harsh and majestic, but at the same time fragile. Have you discovered its wonder and mystery, and has this awareness quickened your spiritual insight and helped you to recognise that of God in everyday life? Rejoice in the splendour of God's continuing Creation.

Be patterns, be examples in all countries, places, islands, nations, wherever you come, that your carriage and life may preach among all sorts of people, and to them; then you will come to walk cheerfully over the world, answering that of God in every one.

George Fox, 1656

www.ingramcontent.com/pod-product-compliance
Lightning Source LLC
Chambersburg PA
CBHW062115040426
42337CB00042B/3680